Original title:
Island in the Sun

Copyright © 2025 Creative Arts Management OÜ
All rights reserved.

Author: Victor Mercer
ISBN HARDBACK: 978-1-80581-606-5
ISBN PAPERBACK: 978-1-80581-133-6
ISBN EBOOK: 978-1-80581-606-5

Golden Horizons Await

Seagulls dive for fries, so bold,
Beach balls bouncing, stories told.
Flip-flops slapping, kids in glee,
A crab scuttles, 'Who's chasing me?'

Sandy castles, moats so wide,
With seashells glued, our parents pride.
Ice cream drips on sun-kissed skin,
Oops! Got some on my chin again.

Solstice Serenade

Bikini tops and summer hats,
Dancing with the lazy cats.
Sunburnt noses, shades askew,
Laughter wraps around like dew.

Surfboards wobble, splashes fly,
A jumping dolphin thinks he's sly.
High-fives echo through the haze,
Triple scoop cones, such sweet malaise.

The Luminescent Coast

Glowsticks glowing, night ignites,
Jellyfish dance in shimmering lights.
Crackers and cheese, picnic delight,
Under the stars, we giggle all night.

Sandy toes and tales so tall,
Got sand in shoes and a ball to stall.
Flip a coin, who gets to dive?
Let's chant the mermaid to come alive!

Echoes of a Summer Breeze

Laughter whispers on the breeze,
Chasing seagulls through the trees.
Sunscreen battles, slippery airs,
Who knew fun could come in pairs?

Kites like fish, they dart and swirl,
An occasional tumble gives a twirl.
Sandy shorts and wet, wild hair,
Catch a wave, if you dare!

A Haven of Warmth

The palm trees dance with glee,
A parrot squawks, 'What's for tea?'
Beach balls bounce with silly grace,
While sunburned tourists start to race.

Flip-flops flying through the air,
Someone's lost their fruity hair!
Sandy toes and laughter loud,
Selfies taken—oh so proud!

Tides of Tranquil Bliss

Crabs in shorts and shades so bright,
Chase each wave with pure delight.
A seagull steals a snack or two,
And dives away, oh what a view!

Sipping drinks adorned with straws,
While sunscreen's dripping down my paws.
Young ones giggle, dig and laugh,
Building castles, oh so daft!

Radiant Shores of Solitude

A beach umbrella flipped around,
A flip-flop victim on the ground.
The sunbaked sand pulls me to stay,
As ocean whispers, "Don't delay!"

Lemons turn to lemonade,
While sun hats flare, a grand parade.
Coconut drinks with tiny straws,
Hiccups caused by summer's cause!

Melodies of the Gentle Tide

Seashells sing a tune so sweet,
While jellyfish dance on little feet.
A surfboard slips, the rider splats,
Adding laughs and friendly chats.

Game of tag with ocean breeze,
Dodging waves, oh what a tease!
With every splash, we holler loud,
Making memories, summery crowd!

Harmonies of Land and Sea

A coconut plays a saxophone,
Shells clap their hands with glee.
Waves dance like it's a party,
While crabs do the cha-cha, you see.

Parrots laugh in the palm trees,
Telling jokes that make me grin.
The sun winks at the ocean,
As sandcastles start to spin.

Seagulls argue over french fries,
They squawk, "No, that fry is mine!"
Dolphins leap, they join the fun,
Making waves and sipping brine.

With flip-flops flying in the air,
And sunscreen on my nose,
The beach becomes a circus show,
Where everything's a funny prose.

Trails of Light on Water

The moon's a disco ball tonight,
Sparkling on the rippling waves.
Fish wear hats and dance around,
While sea turtles spin like knaves.

Stars play hide and seek up high,
The sky giggles, twinkles bright.
Bubbles burst like little laughs,
As crabs hide from the spotlight.

Reflection of a sailor's hat,
Floats by like a silly dream.
A joke was cracked upon the shore,
And the sea began to beam.

Waves carry whispers of delight,
While jellyfish play tambourines.
In this comedy of the night,
Everything's as funny as it seems.

Footprints in the Sunshine

My feet make art upon the sand,
A funny dance, a silly show.
Seagulls steal my lunchtime bread,
As I chase them with a toe.

The sun draws smiles on my face,
While sunshine warms my silly socks.
A crab scuttles to join the race,
With odd-shaped shoes and golden locks.

Neighbors lounge in wacky hats,
Playing cards with wary seagulls.
The game is fierce, but laughter's loud,
As they dodge each other's gulls.

What footprints tell the day's delight?
Each step a giggle, each laugh a cheer.
In the warmth where woes take flight,
The sandy path leads us near.

Kisses of the Morning Glow

Morning beams with teasing rays,
Tickling flowers, spreading cheer.
A turtle yawns and rolls its eyes,
While sipping coffee, loud and clear.

Pancakes land on picnic plates,
Syrup rivers flow with grace.
Ants parade like tiny kings,
In a breakfast race, oh what a chase!

Sunbathers brag about their tan,
While dolphins hop and flip away.
The ocean sings a merry tune,
As laughter chases clouds of gray.

With each kiss the day unfolds,
Jellybeans dance upon the breeze.
In this land where laughter molds,
The morning glow is sure to tease.

Where the Ocean Meets the Light

Seagulls gossip like old friends,
Sandcastles wobble, meet their ends.
The tide rolls in with a cheeky grin,
Kids splashing water, let the fun begin.

Sunscreen applied with a comical sprawl,
Everyone's stuck to the beach like a wall.
A crab with swagger strolls by my feet,
Claiming this sandy realm, oh so sweet.

A game of frisbee crashes like a wave,
Barefoot chases, oh how we misbehave.
Laughter echoes, a contagious delight,
Clumsy ballet in the warm twilight.

With ice creams dripping, we raise a toast,
To memories made, that's what we boast.
The day winds down as the sky turns gold,
Here with my buddies, the best tales told.

Blissful Retreat in Radiant Waters

Tanned bodies, laughing as we float,
Pool noodles twist like a silly boat.
A splash fight rages, no one's exempt,
Who knew that water could be so preempt?

Cocktails slosh, umbrellas in view,
Here comes the waiter, oh what a crew!
Lucky to have this charming escape,
While the sunscreen's melting in a bizarre shape.

Sun hats askew, we dance by the shore,
What's that? A seagull? Oh, the uproar!
Flipping a fish, our dance moves absurd,
Chaos and giggles, it's all quite blurred.

With laughter as sweet as a mango squeeze,
Every moment is ours, with relative ease.
As the sun bows down, we wave goodbye,
To our blissful retreat, we'll surely fly high.

The Caress of Salt and Sun

Salt on my skin, it's a sticky delight,
Trying to balance, I take flight!
A wave crashes in, my hat takes a dip,
Oh what a day! Better grab a grip.

The sun's a comedian, all blinding and bright,
Making silly shadows, what a funny sight!
Turtles swim by, with a curious stare,
"Did you just dive?" "I don't even care!"

Beach volleyball turns into daring drama,
With every missed hit, we burst into a llama.
Laughing so hard, we barely can play,
Who knew that laughing could brighten the day?

As the tide lowers, bringing forth shells,
We trade our stories, our giggles and yells.
The evening rolls in, bringing cool waves,
This life's just too good; oh, how it saves!

Paradise Paints the Evening

Brush strokes of orange paint the sky,
As we chase the last rays with a playful sigh.
Ice cream cones wobble, we're covered in sprinkles,
Grinning like kids with our little crinkles.

A sunset dance, as the waves keep time,
Tripping and tumbling, it's all quite the rhyme.
Flip-flops tossed, our feet in the sand,
We wave to the sun, isn't this grand?

With fireflies glowing, a magical sight,
We gather around, sharing laughs of delight.
The humor of nature; oh what a bore!
When a coconut drops, it starts the uproar.

As shadows stretch longer, we linger and cheer,
Under the stars, with our friends, never fear.
With hearts full of joy, we bid the day night,
In paradise painted, everything feels just right.

Reflections in the Azure Depths

In the water, fish wear crowns,
While crabs dance in velvet gowns.
Seagulls giggle, plotting their schemes,
As I share my sandwich, lost in dreams.

The sun's a jester, bright and bold,
Turns my sunscreen into pure gold.
The waves toss secrets, flip-flop cheer,
Splashing truth and laughter near.

Jellyfish bob like sweet balloons,
While turtles float to silly tunes.
I glance around, the ocean's my stage,
Acting out in a saltwater page.

With sandy toes and salty hair,
I'd trade the world for this sweet air.
So let's toast to naps and long beach days,
Where funny moments dance and play.

Journey to the Heart of Melodies

On a raft made of laughter's song,
We paddle where the mermaids throng.
Each splash a note, a rhythm true,
Creating melodies just for you.

The dolphins play a cheeky game,
Whistling tunes, never the same.
They twirl around in flips and dive,
With seaweed wigs, they come alive.

Turtles ponder their next big joke,
As octopuses giggle, feeling woke.
With every wave, the tunes enhance,
Join the bizarre aquatic dance.

A crab takes center stage with flair,
Telling tales of seaweed hair.
In this buoyant heart, we find delight,
As day drifts onward into night.

Shores of Endless Light

On shores where flip-flops roam the sand,
I find a treasure chest unplanned.
Inside are socks and a rubber duck,
What a lovely, silly stroke of luck!

The sunbeams play hide and seek,
While kids' laughter reaches its peak.
A sandwich flies—oh, what a craze,
As gulls mastering aerial ballet.

Beach balls bounce like happy dreams,
And sunscreen turns into sunny schemes.
Chasing seagulls, we run and race,
With goofy grins on every face.

The horizon dons a golden cap,
While everyone melts in a party nap.
In this glow, we dance and twirl,
On shores where laughter fills the swirl.

Whispering Waves of Radiance

Waves whisper secrets, tales of fun,
Just like a race; who'll be the one?
Saltwater giggles fill the air,
While sunburned poets paint with flair.

A crab with shades walks by with style,
Flipping his claws with kooky guile.
The sun's a jokester, bright and loud,
As beach towels form a silly crowd.

Bikini-clad, the seagulls mooch,
Swiping fries—a clever approach.
While kids build castles, towers so tall,
The ocean's chuckle is a siren's call.

As sunset wraps the day in red,
We can't stop giggling, hearts widespread.
In this paradise where jokes ignite,
The waves laugh gently, a pure delight.

Luminous Landscapes Unfurled

Palm trees sway like they're grooving,
Sunshine dancing, the day improving.
Sandy toes and salty grins,
Seagull squawks, where fun begins.

Beach balls bounce, a playful sight,
Laughter echoes, pure delight.
Flip-flops flying, dodging waves,
Chasing seagulls, like silly knaves.

Dreams Adrift on Gentle Currents

A boat named Soggy Bottom floats,
With crew of clowns in goofy coats.
Navigating with a rubber duck,
Captain laughs, 'Just wish me luck!'

Waves like pillows, soft and round,
Pirates giggle, joy unbound.
Oh, the treasure? Ice cream cones,
Buried under seashell groans.

A Tryst with Warmth and Light

Bikini tops that like to roam,
With shy sunsets they call home.
Sipping drinks that glow like stars,
Hula hoops and chocolate bars.

Ticklish breezes brush the skin,
Watch the sun, it dares to spin.
Snakeskin floaties, laughing loud,
Making waves, we're all so proud.

Where the Sky Kisses the Sea

Surfboards tangled in a heap,
Where ocean dreams and giggles leap.
Clouds like cotton candy spun,
Tickled toes, oh, what fun!

Fishing rods and tangled lines,
Sardines dressed in silly signs.
Waterfights and silly cheers,
Making memories through the years.

Beneath the Whispering Palms

Under palms that sway and dance,
We spot a crab, it takes a chance.
It sidesteps slow, we laugh and cheer,
As it retreats, we hold our beer.

The piña coladas spill like dreams,
While seagulls plot with crafty schemes.
They steal our snacks, we chase in fun,
A sunny day, we'll never shun.

A parrot mimics someone's call,
"Hey! Look at me!" it seems to brawl.
With laughter echoing through the air,
We lose our worries without a care.

So come and join this silly spree,
With sand between toes, wild and free.
Beneath these trees, we'll laugh and play,
In silly games, we'll spend the day.

Hues of Dawn and Dusk

As dawn arrives with golden hues,
We start to dance in silly shoes.
With laughter loud, we swing and sway,
A quirky start to our fine day.

The sunset paints the sky so bright,
We search for crabs with all our might.
They teach us moves that seem so grand,
While we trip on the warm, soft sand.

With drinks in hand and hats askew,
We wave at friends, both old and new.
A shared joke sends us into fits,
As the sunset winks, our laughter flits.

In colors glorious, here we stand,
Chasing mischief, hand in hand.
From dawn to dusk, we'll never fuss,
In this jolly place, it's all a plus.

A Retreat into the Brilliant Unknown

We paddle out on bright blue waves,
With snorkels on, like silly knaves.
A fish swims by, it gives a wink,
In aqua realms, we start to sink.

With sunscreen slathered, we're a sight,
Reflecting smiles in pure delight.
We race a turtle, oh so slow,
While giggles burst like bubbles blow.

Adventurous souls, we dive and roll,
In search of treasures, that's our goal.
Coral castles and seaweed crowns,
Bring out our quirkiest, silliest frowns.

In this weird world, we thrive and roam,
Embracing joy, we find a home.
A brilliant escape where laughter flows,
Our hearts are light, and friendship grows.

Jewel of the Crystal Waters

Waves sparkle like a million lights,
We gather shells, and laughter ignites.
A crab looks up, like "What's the fuss?"
We just can't help but start to cuss.

"Look at that wave!" someone loudly yells,
We slip and slide like rubber gels.
With each splash, our giggles climb,
This silly fun is truly prime.

Floating on floats that fall apart,
We drift in circles, pure works of art.
A dolphin laughs, he joins our spree,
In waters clear, we feel so free.

As sunlight dips to close the day,
We share our tales in funny ways.
This jewel we cherish and adore,
We'll laugh and rinse and laugh some more.

Embrace of the Golden Dawn

The rooster crows a silly tune,
While sleepy heads are still over the moon.
Coffee brews with a quirky fizz,
As socks dance off in an early whiz.

The sun pops up with a wink and a grin,
Making sun hats spin like they're in a din.
Flip-flops clack in a merry parade,
While seaweed tickles, in jests it's laid.

Lemonade stands with goofy signs,
"Free smiles!" they claim, in tangled lines.
A parrot squawks, "I need a laugh!"
While tourists search for their missing calf.

Clouds tumble in a whimsical race,
Creating shadows that frolic with grace.
The golden hues bring giggles a'pride,
As daydreams take us on a funny ride.

Dappled Light on Tropical Leaves

Sunlight dances on the palm tree's skirt,
While ants march in a silly concert.
Lizards make faces; can you believe?
Strutting around like real-life thieves.

Coconut drinks with crazy straws,
A toast to life, with cartoonish jaws.
Vines twist like spaghetti in the breeze,
While monkeys swing, aiming to tease.

Chalky seashells trade their tales,
While crabs do the funky, they don't have fails.
A sandcastle wears a crown askew,
As kids cackle, feeling royal too.

Dappled light whispers a jovial spree,
Inviting laughter, wild and free.
In this realm where smiles recruit,
Nature's humor is oh-so-cute!

Serenity in the Saltair

Waves ripple in a giggling spree,
Carrying tales of a playful sea.
Towels tossed like pizza dough,
While a crab pulls a funny show.

Kites dance high, nearly touching the sky,
As kids run underneath, oh me, oh my!
Shadows chase in a wild embrace,
As seagulls join the silly race.

Dune grass bows in laughter loud,
While a clam dreams of being crowd.
"Hey there!" it shouts in a crusty cheer,
Bringing comical waves that we hold dear.

Saltair's charm brings forth delight,
Under the twinkling of moonlight bright.
In every splash and every giggle,
Life's a joke; let's dance and wiggle!

The Dance of Palm Fronds

Palm fronds shimmy in a breezy boast,
Riding the winds like a laughing ghost.
Coconuts tumble with a playful clink,
Reminding us all not to overthink.

A hammock swings, embracing the air,
As beach balls bounce without a care.
Sunscreen slaps like a winning hand,
While laughter echoes across the sand.

Drinks adorned with tiny umbrellas,
Trade secrets with sunburned fellas.
"Relax!" they say, with ice cream glee,
As the waves whisper sweet jubilee.

The sun dips low, the day does dance,
While flip-flops improvise a chance.
In this realm where humor meets fun,
We twirl and sway until the day is done.

Illuminated Oasis

Bright drinks in our hands, we cheer,
Sipping laughter, nothing to fear.
Seagulls dance above our heads,
While we try on sun hats, all in threads.

Flip-flops flapping, a comical sound,
As we stumble, tripping on the ground.
Palm trees waving, a friendly tease,
Chasing shadows on a warm, gentle breeze.

Sunburnt noses, with silly grins,
We play beach games, let the fun begin!
Laughter echoes, everyone's a clown,
As we roll in the sand, without a frown.

Evenings glow, our tales unfold,
Drifting dreams as the stars turn gold.
In this crazy, cheerful place we've found,
Joy is the treasure, laughter the sound.

The Silent Shoreline

The ocean whispers, secrets trot,
As sand tickles toes, in a funny spot.
Shells play hide and seek, so sly,
We chase after them, oh my, oh my!

Sun hats flopping, we strut and sway,
Trying to dance, but we just betray.
Gulls squawk laughter overhead,
While we juggle snacks, watch 'em spread.

A crab scuttles, with a sassy strut,
And we mimic it, down in the rut.
With laughter bubbling, our hearts unwind,
On this amusing edge, such joy we find.

As the sun dips low, colors ablaze,
We recount our tales in a merry haze.
With goofy grins, closeness we sow,
In this silent haven where laughter flows.

Paradise Found Beyond the Waves

Smooth sailboats glide, waves catch the sun,
Adventure calls, oh, we're on the run!
Bump and bounce, in the salty spray,
Sea turtles laugh as we sail away.

With silly hats and sunscreen applied,
We plunge into blue, joy can't be denied.
Splashing and playing, a silly display,
Even the fish seem to join our play.

Picnics flourish, sandwiches drop,
As seagulls zoom in, we can't make them stop!
Chasing crumbs in a wild, funny spree,
In this quirky realm, we feel so free.

As sunset whispers, bidding adieu,
We'll collect these tales in vibrant hue.
With every chuckle, a memory spins,
In this paradise, laughter never thins.

A Symphony of Dappled Light

Sunshine drips through the swaying leaves,
A playful dance, as nature weaves.
We stumble through patches of bright delight,
With shadows and giggles, our hearts feel light.

In the canopy, we spot a pair,
Of squirrels in tussles, without a care.
We imitate their antics, full of glee,
Chasing each other like us at the sea.

Blankets laid out, snacks in a heap,
While ants march by, the secrets they keep.
Giggling together, we trade silly tales,
As the rhythm of fun in our hearts prevails.

As twilight paints everything gold,
We share our dreams, futures untold.
In this dappled realm where laughter takes flight,
We bask in the magic, a pure delight.

Coconut Dreams and Sandy Toes

Under palm trees, we find our fate,
Coconut drinks that taste first-rate.
Flip-flops squeak; we laugh and grin,
Even the crabs join in our spin.

Sandy toes and a sunburned nose,
Seagulls steal chips as the laughter grows.
Chasing waves, we trip and fall,
Creating memories, we'll cherish all.

Sun hats tilted, don't look so bright,
Yet everyone claims they're a fashion sight.
Tanning lotion? Just a slippery mess,
Still, we apply it, 'cause we're feeling blessed.

Cracking jokes over beach volleyball,
Who needs skills when we're having a ball?
Laughter echoes, echoes through the clear,
Coconut dreams, let's keep them near!

Solitude Beneath Tropical Skies

Tangled in thoughts as the waves recline,
Counting sea turtles, sipping from lime.
A hammock sways like a lazy tune,
Even the sun seems to snooze till noon.

Crabs in my shadow watch with glee,
"Hey, don't you dare walk over me!"
Drifting thoughts amidst salty air,
Where worries vanish, none seem to care.

A lone parrot squawks at the breeze,
"Who cut the cheese?"—oh, such carefree tease!
Umbrellas dance in a whimsical style,
In solitude's grasp, let's bask for a while.

But wait, what's that? A cannonball splash!
A cannonball kid makes a giant crash!
With a laugh at the chaos and splashes all 'round,
Fun beneath skies where peace can be found.

Warmth of the Gentle Current

With sun-kissed cheeks and ties so loose,
We float along, a lazy truce.
The current giggles, whispers, and sways,
Tickling our toes on the sun-drenched bays.

Surfboards line up like ducks in a row,
Who will wipe out? We wait for the show!
Riding the waves, a slippery cheer,
Shouting oaths of "Never again, my dear!"

Banana boats make a splash and a scream,
Life jackets wobbling—oh, what a dream!
Fish fly by with a cheeky grin,
Even the dolphins want to join in.

So raise a laugh to this sunny jest,
In warm waters, let's take a rest.
The gentle current calls to us near,
Where fun and warmth are always sincere!

Radiance on the Water's Edge

Beach towels spread like a colorful quilt,
Who brought the snacks? My hunger's built!
Solar-powered sunscreen, oh what a sight,
Blinding reflections causing comic fright.

Joyful splashes, the children scream,
Taking turns at cannonball extreme.
Full of laughter, we run and slide,
Down the cool slopes where dreams abide.

A seagull lands, eyes on my fries,
With hopes to swoop for a tasty surprise.
We shoo it away, give it the stink eye,
"Get your own lunch, don't even try!"

As sunlight dances like sparkles on glass,
In this playful paradise, time seems to pass.
With giggles and glee, our hearts take flight,
Radiance waits for us, pure day and night!

Elysian Shores

Seagulls laugh, they steal my fry,
A dance of tides, they seem so sly.
Beachballs bounce, but never land,
My sunscreen's lost, in the hot sand.

Flip-flops fly when kites take flight,
I trip on sand, oh what a sight!
My drink's confused, with a little straw,
It's sipping waves, and what a flaw!

Shells tell tales of fishy fights,
Crabs hold court on sandy heights.
A hat of flowers, oh what a mess,
I wear it proud, I must confess.

Umbrella's broken, it's quite a tease,
I chase my drink, blown by the breeze.
With laughter loud, as the sun dips low,
This beach life's fun, I'll gladly show.

Whispers of the Tidal Breeze

Waves crash; they tickle my toes,
Salty air filled with giggles flows.
Tides play tricks on my rubber duck,
It quacks in glee, oh what good luck!

Sandy sandwiches take a nap,
Seagulls plot to steal my wrap.
I wear my shades with a silly grin,
The sun says, "Dance! Just jump right in!"

Bikini mishap, oh what a sight,
My floatie's gone, launched in a flight.
Friends crack jokes, we all just fall,
Chasing laughter, we'll have a ball.

The sun dips low, it starts to glow,
With cheesy jokes we steal the show.
Life's a comedy, when we embrace,
This sandy stage, our happy place.

Embrace of the Golden Horizon

Coconuts drop with a silly thud,
My drink's a mix of rum and mud.
Palm trees sway in a swing-off race,
I try my best to keep up pace.

Sneaky crabs with a dance routine,
They moonwalk sideways, quite the scene!
Flops and splashes, oh what a cheer,
My beach towel's stuck; it's end of year.

A sunburned nose, I'm redder than fire,
Laughter erupts, it fuels my wild desire.
Bumbly bees buzz without a care,
In the sun's embrace, we are a pair.

Snorkels stuck, we float like fish,
Waves crash in, fulfilling each wish.
The day waves goodbye, we laugh and dance,
This golden glow, pure happenstance.

Solstice Serenade

Banana boat rides, a wobbly start,
I splash my friend, it's pure art!
Laughter rises like the ocean foam,
With beach vibes, this is our home.

Sandcastles built with style and flair,
Their walls collapse, who even cares?
A sandy hug, as I tumble down,
Oh, the king of beach clowns wears a crown!

Tanning lotion, a slippery game,
On my snack, it's a very bad claim.
Ice cream drips down my sun-kissed arm,
The sprinkles scatter; oh, what a charm!

As sun sets low, we gather around,
With silly stories, joy's profound.
In this moment, under the sky's hue,
We find our peace, in this merry crew.

A Blog of Light aflame

There once was a crab who could dance,
He pranced on the hot, sandy expanse.
With moves so bizarre,
He claimed he was a star,
And laughed at the sun's silly stance.

His friends joined in with their own flair,
A sea turtle wearing a plaid chair.
They twirled and they spun,
Underneath all the fun,
With laughter echoing through the air.

Then came a fish, with a flashy bow tie,
Who proclaimed, "I'm the catch of the pie!"
He juggled some shells,
And everyone yells,
"Let's feast 'til we float to the sky!"

The tide rolled in, but they remained bright,
Beneath a sky painted cheerful and white.
In a whirl of delight,
Their worries took flight,
As day turned to magical night.

Days of Dreaming in Sunlight

In a land where coconuts play,
And monkeys do yoga all day,
The sun wears a grin,
While waves make a din,
As surfboards on rooftops sway.

A parrot squawks jokes from a tree,
Cracking up all the folks at sea.
With a splash and a roll,
He's stolen the show,
While sunhats spin round with glee.

Kids build sand castles so tall,
With moats filled with fish—what a ball!
But a sneaky crab,
Gives a playful jab,
Knocking down their fort with a call.

As day pools in hues of bright gold,
And stories of laughter unfold,
They weave a grand tale,
With humor in sail,
In dreams where the sun never grows old.

Enchanted Realms of Radiance

In a place where the coconuts giggle,
A flamingo does quite the wiggly wiggle.
He pulls silly pranks,
With the help of the banks,
Where the sun beams create a tease and a jiggle.

The waves tell tall tales to the shore,
Of turtles who dance and ignore.
They shimmy and slide,
In the deep, they confide,
While crabs drum a beat to encore.

A pineapple hat on a sea otter's head,
Dances round like it's living instead.
With friends all around,
In laughter they're bound,
Under skies that are sunny and red.

As twilight whispers secrets of fun,
They dream of adventures begun.
In laughter's embrace,
They find their own place,
Where the magic of joy is a run.

Reflections of a Sunlit Retreat

On this sandy spot where I lay,
A crab stole my sandwich and scampered away.
My drink's a bit salty, what can I say?
Yet laughter floats softly; it brightens the day.

The seagulls are squawking, quite full of sass,
Chasing my flip-flops while I take a pass.
They dive for a snack, oh what a class,
If only my sunscreen could stop this sun's brass.

My friend caught a fish or so he claimed,
But all we caught was a sunburn, untamed.
We grinned like the rays, not feeling all shamed,
'Twas the beach's own glow that left us inflamed.

As dusk falls gently, we sit with our drinks,
And ponder our lives with its giggles and kinks.
The epitome of fun as each moment winks,
In a world full of joy, there's no time to think.

The Harmony of Palms and Waves

Underneath the palms, I lounge so proud,
While mosquitoes hum like a hyperactive crowd.
The waves crash gently with a thundering sound,
I think they're just dancing, not to be drowned.

My hat flies away, a bold gust in play,
I chase it with laughter, what else can I say?
A sun-kissed adventure unfolds every day,
While sunscreen and giggles are never cliché.

My toes dig in sand like magical treasure,
Each grain tells a story, providing great measure.
I sip on a coconut, that golden old pleasure,
And dance with the waves, it's a topic for leisure.

As daylight is fading, the fun doesn't stop,
With friends by my side, we chant like a prop.
In this quirky cocoon, we clearly won't swap,
Here laughter ignites and we'll never just drop.

Rhythms of the Sea and Sky

Waves roll in rhythms, a jubilant beat,
While I try to dance with my two left feet.
A dolphin waves back from his watery seat,
And I just might tackle this sea-pumpkin treat.

My friend shouts with glee as he takes a big fall,
The sand is surprisingly soft after all.
We plot our next antics through giggles and squall,
With this daily mischief, we'll stand proud and tall.

Each splash of the tide makes us howl out in fun,
As the sun starts its dip, we forget we've begun.
A limbo contest breaks out, who'll be the one?
To stumble and fumble, till we're all on the run.

With twilight upon us, the stars start to gleam,
We share silly stories; it's all like a dream.
Laughter rings out as we plot our regime,
For tomorrow brings mischief, or so it will seem.

Gilded Moments at Dusk

As the day takes its bow, the sun starts to blend,
With hues of gold dancing, like a good friend.
The sand becomes cooler, as the giggles ascend,
Each moment a treasure, with joy we pretend.

My hat's on the grill; it's a picturesque sight,
And old surfboards lean, with a touch of delight.
While starfish applaud in their own quiet night,
We feast on hotdogs and toast with our might.

The stars peek above, like kids in the dark,
With fireflies buzzing to create their spark.
We roast marshmallows, though some go in the park,
And laughter erupts, pressing peace to our hearts.

So here's to the moments, the funny and bright,
Where friendships grow strong when the world feels just right.
In joyous surrender, we bask in the light,
For gilded tomorrows await just in sight.

Melodies of the Horizon

Seagulls squawk and steal my fries,
The sun is high, oh, what a surprise!
I wear a hat that's far too wide,
And sunburned toes I cannot hide.

The waves come in with a cheeky grin,
They splash my drink, oh where to begin?
My friend just fell while trying to dance,
Now he's covered in sand - no chance!

We chase the crabs with giggles loud,
They scuttle fast, they're so darn proud.
A beach ball flies, then hits a guy,
He laughs it off, oh my, oh my!

As sunset paints the sky so bright,
I dream of snacks and a nap tonight.
The moon will rise, with stars in tow,
Tomorrow's fun, just steal the show!

Reveries by the Bright Cove

Lemonade spills down the slide so slick,
My belly flop was quite the trick.
Sandcastles built with flair and pride,
But waves come in, they take the tide.

Turtles wear shades, they think they're cool,
While I dive in, just like a fool.
Flip-flops flying in every direction,
Surfboards glide with no affection.

Picnics end in a food fight feast,
Flying ants join in, at least!
A sunburned nose, a goofy laugh,
We'll swim and play, that's our epitaph.

The sun dips low, the day must go,
But we'll be back, that much we know.
Bright cove memories stuck in our heads,
Like sticky ketchup with crusty breads!

Beyond the Glimmering Blue

Dancing shells that tap their feet,
We join the rhythm, oh what a treat!
Mermaids giggle, they hold their breath,
We splash around, no hint of death.

Flavors of coconut and pineapple fun,
Sticky fingers when we're on the run.
A volcano cake, it's hard to eat,
With melting candles, what a sweet feat!

Seashells sing with voices loud,
While we attempt to join the crowd.
Every wave a laugh or two,
Funny how sunburns make us blue.

But as the stars begin to tease,
We share our secrets, starlit breeze.
The moon is our guide, in the cool dark night,
Making funny faces, everything feels right!

Escape to the Fragrant Sea

With fruity drinks and silly hats,
We parade around like clumsy cats.
A piña colada spills on my shoes,
With a giggle, I'll never refuse.

Sun-kissed cheeks and wearied eyes,
Salty laughter fills the blue skies.
We race the wind, with kites in tow,
But tangled strings steal the show, oh no!

Shells and treasures washed ashore,
Discovering crabs we can't ignore.
A dance-off with a jellyfish crew,
They wobble and sway, we join them too!

As twilight weaves a twinkling thread,
We spin memories, the laughter spread.
With a promise to return next week,
For sunshine moments, that's what we seek!

Nectar of the Swaying Palms

Beneath the dancing palms so bright,
A squirrel tried to steal my drink last night.
He wore a tiny hat, quite absurd you see,
Claiming he was out for a tropical spree.

I laughed so hard, my juice did spill,
As he twirled around, a thrill-seeking thrill.
He chattered on about fruit and fun,
Oh, what a night for a squirrel on the run!

Sandcastles built with sandy glee,
But my flip-flop sunk, oh woe is me!
A crab moved in, made it his throne,
While I stood there, feeling alone!

Yet in this seaside circus, we forgot the strife,
With every wave crashing, we celebrated life.
A fruity punch, a splashy dive,
Who knew a night could feel so alive?

Captured in a Dreamlike Glow

In twilight's glow, the fish all dance,
Chasing shadows, they take a chance.
A seagull squawked, "Hey, watch my moves!"
Belly flops and backflips, he really grooves!

My floaty got snagged by a sneaky wave,
The ocean chuckled, what a knave!
I flailed about, like a fish out of sea,
While seaweed wrapped like a movie spree!

Sipping coconuts, feeling like kings,
Riding the tide on inflatable swings.
The sun dipped low, painting the sky,
And our laughter echoed, oh, me oh my!

As night arrived, the crabs took charge,
Hosting a dance party, it felt so large.
"Join in my conga!" one crab did shout,
With all my heart, I couldn't back out!

Mornings Aglow with Tranquility

The rooster crowed, a clumsy bugle,
While I tripped over my towel so frugal.
A yoga pose? I toppled right down,
With laughter ringing, I wore a frown!

The sun peeked out with a cheeky grin,
While sipping coffee, I nearly fell in.
Splashing everywhere was quite the scene,
Am I a coffee drinker or a coffee bean?

Bouncing on waves like a little pup,
A dolphin splashed, "Hey, wanna wake up?"
I waved my arms like a crazy bird,
He jumped so high, my giggles stirred!

In the morning light, the fun begins,
With pet crabs juggling their shiny fins.
We danced barefoot on the warm, soft sand,
In this serene spot, laughter is grand!

Secrets of the Clementine Bay

Where waves whisper secrets and stories shared,
A turtle rolled by, a bit unprepared.
"Oh hey, watch my shell!" he gave a shout,
While flipping over, without a doubt!

The jellyfish glowed like bulbs at night,
But touched one once, and oh what a fright!
I danced and spun like a dizzy kite,
Saying, "Next time, just keep out of sight!"

Sandwiches flying, picnics gone wild,
As gulls swooped down, oh look, they smiled.
They took my lunch; I chased them in vain,
But they quacked back like it was a game!

Yet in this bay, where giggles prevail,
We share these moments, our laughter won't fail.
With sun on our faces and smart jokes galore,
In these salty waters, we all want more!

Celestial Sands Beneath Our Feet

Barefoot we trudge, our toes in the silt,
Laughter erupts, like the waves that we built.
Umbrellas topple, drinks spill on the ground,
Seagulls squawking, like jesters, they hound.

With sunscreen slathered, we fashion our gear,
A dance-off erupts while the sun's drawing near.
The sand's a comedian, tickling our toes,
We stumble and tumble, oh, how kinship grows!

An iguana judges, perched on a rock,
As we strike our best poses, he's in for a shock.
A crab joins the fun, with a sideways prance,
In the theater of beach, we all take a chance.

Lively the air is, with giggles and glee,
While sunbeams conspire to warm you and me.
With salt in our hair and mud on our feet,
Life's a carnival, so grand and so sweet!

Daydreams over Coral Reefs

Flippers in hand, we dive down to play,
Mermaids and dolphins have come out to sway.
Underwater ballet, we twirl with the fish,
A sea cucumber joins, oh, what a dish!

Splashing and giggling, we drift with the tide,
While turtles roll by, they laugh and abide.
A quest for treasures, we shoveled with glee,
Only to find a shoe? Oh, is that from me?

The coral is painted in hues like a dream,
As fish make their jokes, and the sea starts to beam.
A clownfish winks, and we're all in his jest,
Who needs a crown when you're diving with the best?

With bubbles like candles, our laughter does soar,
Each splash is a song, who could ask for more?
As we float to the surface, with giggles we gleam,
The ocean's our stage, the sun's our regime!

Reflections on a Liquid Horizon

Waves crash like laughter, a chorus so bright,
We balance on surfboards, what a silly sight!
With every wipeout, we shriek and we roll,
Each splash is a story, a dive for the soul.

Fish flip in circles as if in a race,
While we chase the currents, we're off with no trace.
Their gills flap with joy, it's a competition,
As we wave from our boards, what a fun rendition!

Reflection's a joker, it teases our gaze,
We smile at the waves in this sunlit haze.
In the water, we're floating, our worries all flee,
As fins and feet mingle in a dance so carefree.

With horizons a canvas, we paint with our shouts,
In this carnival sea, there are no doubts.
It's laughter we cling to, in each playful wake,
On this liquid stage, oh, what joy we make!

Sunlit Sanctuary

Under the sun, a hammock we find,
Swinging and chatting, with laughter combined.
A lemonade fountain and jokes shared on cue,
We toast to the day, with a big, cheesy crew.

Palm fronds dance lightly, a breeze lifts our hair,
As we plot our next prank with a mischievous flair.
Tiki torches flicker, the night's drawing near,
While shadows do jiggle, we grin ear to ear.

The stars start to twinkle, our bonfire does crack,
Tales of our mischief, we're never looking back.
With marshmallows roasting, we scheme and we plot,
Who knew our fun could be captured like this spot?

And as night deepens, we sing loud and bold,
In our sunlit retreat, where stories unfold.
With friends all around, and the moon shining bright,
We dance in the dark, igniting the night!

Reflections in a Crystal Lagoon

Gazing at fish with their silly little grins,
Bubbles dance joyfully, where the laughter begins.
A frog in a top hat, quite ready to sing,
Steals the show with his leaps and a splishy-splash fling.

Sipping on cocktails with umbrellas so bright,
Coconuts giggle, what a funny sight!
Sunburned tourists bobbing like ducks,
While seagulls tell jokes about their clumsy luck.

Clowns on the shore juggling jellyfish,
Each flop and each wiggle—a captivating wish.
The tide plays the drums, oh what a parade,
As we dance with the crabs in their sandy charade.

A crab with a monocle is telling a tale,
Of ships that are pirates, and fish that can sail.
With snacks on our laps and big hats on our heads,
We laugh till we cry, while the lobster just spreads.

Swelling Waves of Euphoria

Riding the waves, all dressed up like clowns,
Flip-flops are flying, as laughter abounds.
A dolphin in shades does a flip with great flair,
While I chase my beach hat all over the air.

Sunscreen on noses, we look like bizarre,
Yet each splash we make is a total rockstar!
Bikini-clad seagulls sing songs of the shore,
We join in just before we all tumble and roar.

The tide brings a treasure: a shoe made of cheese,
Delightfully weird, we can't help but tease.
A crab steals my sandwich, but I laugh and I grin,
For it's not every day you outrun a sea-kin!

Like surfing in bubbles, we glide with great grace,
Through waves of sheer joy, there's no need to race.
Let's toast with our sodas, let the chuckles unfurl,
For every odd moment is a victory whirl!

Sweet Whispers in the Breeze

The wind tells a secret—it tickles my nose,
With whispers of laughter, where mischief just grows.
A squirrel on a surfboard glides with such style,
Wearing sunglasses, he's got the best smile!

Picnics on the grass with ants making haste,
To steal away crumbs, oh, what a wee chase!
I fumble my sandwich, it lands in the sand,
But we giggle away—we're too happy to land!

The parrot's a comedian with jokes of his own,
He roasts all the tourists, the seeds he has sown.
With each silly quip, we howl and we cheer,
As the sun winks at us, it's perfectly clear.

We race with the breeze, our laughter cascades,
On this merry retreat where the joy never fades.
A game of charades with the waves at our feet,
Unraveling laughter—it's simply a treat!

Shimmering Skies Above

Balloons in the sky are our fluffy friends,
They bob and they weave, on their joy it depends.
With kites of all colors, we twist and we twirl,
As the sun plays peek-a-boo, we skip and we whirl.

A raccoon in shades is DJing the fun,
With beats that get everyone's toes on the run.
We dance with a crab who leads with great flair,
His rhythm infectious, we've no worries or care.

The clouds are just cotton, they fluff up the scene,
As I chase after giggles, to feel so serene.
A banana peel slips, watch me tumble and drop,
As laughter erupts, we just can't get enough!

So here's to the moments when life's full of glee,
Where funny and silly collide with the sea.
With stars in our eyes and smiles ever bright,
Together we'll shine through the long, balmy night.

Lullabies of a Sheltered Cove

In a cove where coconuts sway,
Seagulls squawk, they sing all day.
Turtles bask in sunlit bliss,
Whispering secrets, they can't resist.

Crabs do the cha-cha on the shore,
While fish play tag — oh, what a score!
Waves giggle as they tickle toes,
Joy is found where the laughter grows.

The palm trees wear sunglasses so bright,
Chilling out, what a glorious sight!
Sandcastles rise, then fall with a sigh,
As clumsy kids lose their dreams in the tide.

So grab a drink, let worries fade,
Join the dance in this fun parade.
With each splash and silly cheer,
Life's a laugh in this paradise here.

Sunbeams and Seafaring Wishes

Sunbeams leap on the waves' crest,
While sailors nap, they feel quite blessed.
A mermaid mugs for a selfie glance,
Flipping her tail in a cheeky dance.

Pirates juggle fish, what a sight!
Dressed in sarongs, they're feeling bright.
Seagulls steal chips from a picnic spread,
Laughing as folks toss crumbs instead.

The breeze tells tales of mischief grand,
Of sock-stealing crabs on shifting sand.
Watermelon smiles, sugary fun,
Every splash is a wordless pun.

So gather your friends, don your hats,
Chase the sun where the humor's at.
In this world where giggles fly,
Life's a joke beneath the blue sky.

Lullabies of a Sheltered Cove

In a cove where coconuts sway,
Seagulls squawk, they sing all day.
Turtles bask in sunlit bliss,
Whispering secrets, they can't resist.

Crabs do the cha-cha on the shore,
While fish play tag — oh, what a score!
Waves giggle as they tickle toes,
Joy is found where the laughter grows.

The palm trees wear sunglasses so bright,
Chilling out, what a glorious sight!
Sandcastles rise, then fall with a sigh,
As clumsy kids lose their dreams in the tide.

So grab a drink, let worries fade,
Join the dance in this fun parade.
With each splash and silly cheer,
Life's a laugh in this paradise here.

Sunbeams and Seafaring Wishes

Sunbeams leap on the waves' crest,
While sailors nap, they feel quite blessed.
A mermaid mugs for a selfie glance,
Flipping her tail in a cheeky dance.

Pirates juggle fish, what a sight!
Dressed in sarongs, they're feeling bright.
Seagulls steal chips from a picnic spread,
Laughing as folks toss crumbs instead.

The breeze tells tales of mischief grand,
Of sock-stealing crabs on shifting sand.
Watermelon smiles, sugary fun,
Every splash is a wordless pun.

So gather your friends, don your hats,
Chase the sun where the humor's at.
In this world where giggles fly,
Life's a joke beneath the blue sky.

The Allure of Luminous Horizons

Oh, the horizon glows so divine,
Where silliness and sunshine intertwine.
Fish are pulling pranks with delight,
Diving for laughs, oh, what a sight!

Glowworms join for a disco night,
Wiggling to a tune that feels just right.
The wind whispers jokes, cheekily bold,
As crabs crack up, their stories told.

A starfish asks, "Why don't we dive?"
"Because we might just be too alive!"
Laughter dances on the evening waves,
Feeling alive, no one misbehaves.

So raise your glass, toast to the skies,
With every laugh, joy multiplies.
In this place where the sunsets glow,
Funny moments, forever they'll flow.

Echoes of the Surging Tide

The tide rolls in with a bubbly cheer,
Whispers of waves tickle the ear.
Seashells hold giggles from the deep,
Their secrets shared that never sleep.

Dolphins dance like wiggly stars,
Making impressions like little bizarre.
Flip-flops toss in the thick soft sand,
Who knew this place could be so grand?

The sun dips low, its canvas wide,
Painting the sky where memories hide.
Crackers and cheese, what a fine spread,
As we laugh 'til the moon's overhead.

So let the waves carry your fears,
Join the laughter and joyful cheers.
In every splash, a story to tell,
Echoes of fun, cast under the spell.

Odes to the Day's Embrace

In a land where laughter sails,
The seagulls dance with playful tales.
Fruits like suns on trees do swing,
While monkeys plan their daring fling.

Sun hats wobble, drinks spill wide,
While beach balls race, we take a ride.
Flip-flops squeak with every stride,
And all worries drift like the tide.

Kites catch breezes, colors clash,
Sunburned noses in a flash.
We search for treasures, make a mess,
Our giggles echo, pure success.

As the day bids us goodnight,
Stars poke through, a stunning sight.
With sand in shoes, we dance away,
In dreams of joy, we'll laugh and play.

Celestial Wonders at the Shore

The sky wears blue with fluffy fluff,
We build our castles, not too tough.
Waves crash down, a sloshy game,
While sandcastles earn us fame.

Turtles peek with toothy grins,
As children squeal, the fun begins.
Shells as trophies claim our prize,
Silly faces, bright, surprise.

Surfboards wobble, laughter reigns,
Each tumble brings no lasting pains.
With ice cream drips and sticky hands,
We scribble dreams in shifting sands.

As the day turns golden hue,
We wave goodbye, the stars shine through.
Tomorrow's whispers softly tease,
For fun awaits with every breeze.

Tranquility Beneath Sunlit Canopies

Beneath the leaves, the laughter flows,
With lemonade and silly prose.
Picnic mats and ants in line,
The sun makes everything divine.

Games of tag with friendly shouts,
Round and round, the joy, no doubts.
Bouncing balls and giggly pairs,
In this wonder, we lose our cares.

Clouds drift by, they dance and play,
While we enjoy this bright buffet.
Coconuts that wear a grin,
Say let the fun and games begin!

As shadows stretch, we gather close,
With stories shared and silly boasts.
This day of joy, we'll hold so tight,
In sunlit shades, we end the night.

The Echoing Call of Adventure

A treasure map? We're on the hunt,
With pirate hats and a cheeky grunt.
X marks the spot, we dig with glee,
What treasures lie beneath the sea?

Our boats made of laughter, highs and lows,
With crew so bold, anything goes.
The compass spins, we laugh, we cheer,
With every wave, adventure near.

Jellyfish dance, and dolphins play,
Our spirits soar, we yell "hooray!"
Snorkels on, we gawk at fish,
In every splash, a bubbling wish.

As sun dips low, the sky ablaze,
We trade our tales of daring days.
With every heartbeat, the same refrain,
Adventure calls, we'll come again!

Cradled by Light and Laughter

The warmth of rays, a cozy hug,
We lounge in shade with snacks to chug.
Silly games with goofy friends,
In every giggle, the fun never ends.

Hats that fly and drinks that spill,
Joyful chaos, a carefree thrill.
We race the waves, we splash and shout,
With every jump, there's no doubt.

Sunset symphonies, colors bled,
With sleepy yawns, we head to bed.
But in our dreams, we'll still embrace,
The laughter that time cannot erase.

Morning awaits, bright and clear,
With new adventures drawing near.
In every heart, a warmth we keep,
Cradled by light, as night drifts to sleep.

Parading Colors of the Dusk

The sky puts on a vibrant show,
As colors dance, the breezes flow.
Seagulls squawk with silly flair,
While folks juggle their sun-kissed hair.

Tanned tourists toast with goofy glee,
In flip-flops chasing every bee.
Laughter spills with each sunset's hue,
As the sand gets stuck on our shoes.

Bikinis clash like paint that drips,
While sunburned noses dance and flip.
Umbrellas twirl like disco lights,
As the day bids farewell to the nights.

With every wave, a laugh erupts,
Who knew the tide had such hoopla?
As dusk fades into tales of fun,
We grin and cheer, our hearts now won.

Embraces Wrapped in Warmth

In hammocks swaying, we toast with joy,
Sipping sweet drinks as if we're coy.
With every chuckle and snort of glee,
We cuddle closely, just you and me.

The sun wraps us in a golden hug,
While sand sticks on like a playful bug.
We laugh as we trip over our toes,
As each delightful mishap just grows.

Coconuts roll like round, silly moons,
While sun hats take off like wayward balloons.
Laughter erupts at the silliest sights,
As we bask in the warmth, oh what delights!

With warm embraces and joyful cheers,
We dance with sandcastles, forget our fears.
Together we share this amusing spree,
Wrapped in laughter, just you and me.

A Voyage of Serenity

A tiny boat bobs along with cheer,
As we capture memories, oh so dear.
The captain sneezes, tipping us all,
While fish swim by, just witnessing the fall.

With hats afloat and sandals askew,
We navigate waters, a clownish crew.
The breeze teases with a playful grip,
As we sail along on this goofy trip.

Seagulls squawk, singing silly tunes,
While jellyfish waltz beneath the moons.
We wave to dolphins, who wink and glide,
As laughter bubbles, we hold the tide.

With every swell, a ticklish thrill,
This voyage beckons, our hearts to fill.
A journey so merry, we float, we sway,
In this wacky world, we choose to play.

The Ocean's Golden Embrace

The waves crash down like a comical scene,
As kids run wild, chasing their dreams.
With splashes and giggles, the fun just grows,
What a mess made by water from toes!

Sandy bottoms and sunscreen galore,
While seagulls dance, craftily they soar.
A sunburned lobster struts by with glee,
To find a matching hat — oh, fancy free!

Floating on blubber, a whimsical ride,
While beach balls bounce and spirits collide.
With each goofy trick, we double the fun,
As the sun dips low — our day's just begun.

In this embrace of laughter and light,
We savor each moment, day turns to night.
With our ocean tales forever alive,
We'll reminisce joy, together we thrive.

www.ingramcontent.com/pod-product-compliance
Lightning Source LLC
Chambersburg PA
CBHW072132070526
44585CB00016B/1644